The Beagle Clowr

STORY TELLI

Remember your Beagle is only a heartbeat at your side

Susan McNeil

the founder of the

Bizarte Beagle

THE BEAGLE

A Survival Handbook essential to Beagle ownership.

The guidance in this book is based on rearing and the training of the Beagle but would be suitable for other breeds of dogs.

Included in this manuscript are short stories from developing a Breeding Kennels, also Rearing and Showing for over 30 years ... ...

Editor's Note:

Whilst transferring Susan's words of rearing and training Beagles into book form, I started to understand clearer our Jack Russell, her needs and moods.

I recommend this book to all lovers of their four legged companions or 'Furkids' as Susan calls them. Whether to train them or to know them and their needs a little better.

STORY TELLING THIRTY NINE

THE BEAGLE

CLOWN OF THE DOG WORLD.

BY

Susan McNeil

Acknowledgements:
Must go to my Pack of Bizarte Beagles,
my owners, past and present who
have become friends that inspired me to
write this book.

THE BEAGLE

ISBN 978 1 9162712 5 8

Published by

Percychatteybooks Publisher

Content

PREFACE==

My first Beagle was chosen by my family when I was 12. He was a Tan and White pedigree named Ozzy, but he had no KENNEL CLUB Registration or at least I don't remember.

We had gone to a Kennels to visit and choose a puppy. Mother was after a Pekingese Corgi (like the Queens) or a Pyrenees Mountain Dog! We came home with a male Beagle Puppy! It was a sign. Some 25 years later I decided to go ahead and look for a Beagle for myself now I had a home and horses, living in the Sussex Countryside.

From a kennel which was advertised in a County Newspaper I became the owner of Fairwinds Tan, a bitch, which I showed and who accompanied me on my hacks out on my horse.

After years of showing horses the doggy showing was very similar, after all it's all about producing the best animal on the day.

I enjoyed her as a friend, also the showing her at different shows. So I decided on another Beagle and was joined with a Bitch from Annavah kennel, she became my foundation bitch named Prudence breeding my own show puppy, a bitch, and then my 'Bizarte' affix was born Bizarte Angelic. I attended some Championship shows and had some success but actually preferred the Companion Shows because the people were so friendly and more relaxed.

I gained many awards and had lots of fun as did my Beagles. I had foaled mares so breeding came easily to me. I became an Assured Breeder through the KENNEL CLUB, and also a member of Shoreham and Haywards Heath Ringcraft clubs. I judged at dog and horse shows.

When I moved to Spain later with my Pack, I became a Judge for many Charity shows and worked with a few dog charities obtaining monies to save the stray and unwanted dogs.

There I loved to show too at the CH. Shows and was a member of the RSCE of Espania
and gained many awards including Group wins. Now I live in France with my Pack and enjoying retirement.

I have given advice freely about Beagles when asked, which has proved helpful through the years for people, although your
vet is the best source of medical aid.

I organised group walks, the one on Cissbury Ring in Sussex had 50 Beagles and their proud owners joined in.

We (the pack) often did film work, Lloyds Bank Commercial shoot in Blue Sky Studios London.

Roberto Cavalli, Dress Designer (interesting to see him holding 5 Beagles whilst smoking a big fat cigar!) in Chelsea, Vanity Fair in Germany,

Fashion shoots at Led Zeppelin's old stately home, also various others including 'Beagle Street Insurance' shot in Fulham studios.

All of my puppies were health tested and carried the FCI Affix Bizarte Beagles. They are all over the world including Tokyo, Ibiza, Tenerife, Italy and Spain.

Over the years My experience still holds true as I still have 4 Beagles and get asked daily for help in all matters relating to Beagles.

Chapter One

The search can begin ... .

So you want to be owned by a Beagle? A Great choice.

Now is the time to learn about the breed before you make that purchase. Here in this book I aim to assist you from choosing your puppy, nurturing, training, health and exercise.

It is vital that you learn all you can prior to purchase thus making the whole process easier for you and your new puppy, and the experience is not so daunting. The more knowledge you have the more prepared you are for surprises should they occur.

So ... the most important decision is finding the right breed in the beginning for you and your family of any dog, and in choosing The Beagle I will only discuss that breed within these pages, and your puppy will be referred to as 'He/she'.

Your puppy will be a member of your family and can live for up to 16 years of age so your new 'Fur kid' must fit in with you, your partner and children, also your lifestyle. And let's not forget extended family too as they may well be called upon to puppy sit occasionally.

All breeds need attention training and therefore a back-up of money, also your time so if you cannot commit now is the time to wait until you can! Getting a puppy will be an expensive outlay but look at it like this, buy cheap ... buy twice ... normally it will be true, so understand that it is like an investment and divide the outlay in years that your Beagle will hopefully live, you will reap the rewards.

Truly there is no such thing as a 'Bargain' in the dog world - you may end up spending a small fortune on veterinary fees etc or have to pass the dog on to a rescue centre if his temperament is not right to be around you, your children! and other pets. I cannot over emphasize the word 'Temperament' crucial to get right and in choosing a Beagle from a reputable breeder you will have the history and can ask all about the lineage.

So you have read many books on the breed, and Googled about them, maybe joined a Beagle Group on Social media, or your friend has one and so on.

If possible go and spend some time with them or join a Beagle meet up where like minded owners take their precious Beagles for playtime in an enclosed arena. Visit the local shows or Championship shows where you can meet owners with the Beagle in the ring and talk to them after their classes, most of these folks are breeders themselves so you can find out first-hand. There will be a list of shows

Companion and Champ shows on the KENNEL CLUB site.

Talk to those folks, they have the reality or go to a Doggy Day Care Centre, there are usually ones within your town and see how they act. Also go onto the KENNEL CLUB website and search for Beagle Breeders, usually they are only too happy to talk to you and answer any questions you may have. Perhaps you can then go on a waiting list with your chosen Breeder, so you will be able to find information about the Breed and what they should look like, in other words true to the Breed.

Buying a Beagle puppy from a reputable breeder you should expect to pay in excess of £1000. You may say well I don't want to show it or breed so why not get one from Joe down the road for £300?

When buying from a Good Breeder who is recognised by the KENNEL CLUB your money will be buying a puppy that has been carefully bred, true to type and from great parentage. It's not a case of sticking a male and female together in the back yard … we call these folk (Backyard Breeders) it is a thought process ensuring the best outcome for the puppies born, so both dogs tested for health problems, both have wonderful temperaments and are raised in the correct environment.

In a healthy practice they have also come from a good line that is their genetic history, the temperament is all important. No good having a fabulous looking dog which becomes 'difficult' in all situations.

Temperaments are bred not made and as you may see the Dam and the Sire you can assess the situation clearer. Listen to the Breeder does she sound enthusiastic and knowledgeable? If you are not seeking a puppy then again, your breeder may have an older Beagle, one that has been retired from the ring and breeding duties.

Love Is ... ...
Nothing as cute as a mischievous Beagle Puppy

Or differently, charities may have one available, some dogs for re-homing, including a 'Beagle Welfare' but do remember there will be a criteria you must attain or the temperament or any Vices may not be fully known, in other words 'there is no history.'

Breeders can be found on several sites on your PC, the KENNEL CLUB, as I mentioned is only one. Here there will be names and addresses and their e-mail or telephone numbers and how they world like to be contacted. Look closely and you will see who has a litter now ready for their new homes.

Also, and importantly, you will find some breeders have a badge of recognition as an Assured Breeder. These are awarded to breeders who comply with rules laid down by the KENNEL CLUB, and have been visited and questioned with all answers on forms (which can take several hours to read). You can read more about this on the KENNEL CLUB site.

They test all Beagles which are used for breeding with DNA samples, which are sent off for health testing prior to mating so that their puppies will not be affected. Your vet cannot do these tests as they are done by a specialist.

It is for the breeder to send cheek swabs off to specialist laboratories to check for certain diseases appertaining to Beagles such as, MLS, FV11, , NCCD and Lafora ... (you can read about these on 'www.beaglehealth' on the web)

Also a breeder's premises will have to undergo a check from Assured Breeder agents from the KENNEL CLUB to make sure the home or kennels comply with good ethics i.e. cleanliness, warmth, food even down to a thermometer and fire extinguisher if there are kennels outside. If you find a breeder who is regularly producing litters, then a Licence is also required from their local Council. You can ask to see these documents.

Licences and certificates are given to the Breeder, with the former showing the outfit is up to standard. (I used to frame mine and have them visible on the wall). My Licences to trade as a breeder, my Assured Breeder Certificate, Affix Certificate, and, Club memberships all nicely framed in itself giving new clients confidence. Accolades can also be given, and these are shown on the KENNEL CLUB site.

You will also find sites that advertise puppies for sale, such as 'Pets 4 Homes' they use photographs as well as their web site link. There are a few sites like these and a good Breeder will stand out from the bad, you must look closely ... does it say the tests are done?

There are many questions, does it say you can see puppies with their Mum? Do the puppies resemble the breed definition picture on the KENNEL CLUB site? Do they come with papers are they then registered with the KENNEL CLUB? Are they at a genuine address? Is this breeder a member of the KENNEL CLUB? If they are advertising as being an Assured breeder then they world be listed on the KENNEL CLUB site as such.

The site is not bad in itself and it is free to advertise, so any advertising portal for a Breeder is good as long as it is genuine. Please be aware that the price also reflects the quality and you may say 'well I don't want to show the puppy so I don't care if there are no papers, or health tests ... it is cheap, I want it'. I world say Do not throw good money to bad ... there are Puppy Farms and they still exist.

Some may not resemble this but look like a normal house and will have puppies to show you maybe in a stable or even a car park layby or their home IT IS then Buyer Beware ... so many get caught by this.

This is a Large Puppy Farm ...
... AVOID at all costs

The Beagle Club of Great Britain will also have lists of good breeders. It is like most animal purchases. 'Buyer Beware' ... if in doubt find out as much as you can. Interestingly I found one advertisement years ago that was using a photo I had taken of 'MY' puppies, so you see how tricksters work! If in doubt step away.

A good breeder will have an Affix. This is a pre-name before or after the name of the puppy. This has to be registered in the country of residence. Mine are Bizarte and is included in the name of the dog.

Not all puppies for sale will have an Affix . They can still be registered with the KENNEL CLUB as long as the parents are as well. Fees have to be paid to the governing body for the Affix registration. KENNEL CLUB also registers each puppy. So those folks who think its easy money, it ain't!

If the puppies are genuinely registered with the KENNEL CLUB it means that they come from parentage who have also been registered, there will be a line of breeding going back to grandparents, great grandparents and so on.

In other words, a PEDIGREE is usually 4 or 5 generations, this being the case it is possible to search through the Pedigree Data base the history of your puppy.

This will be useful to know that your puppy has a Pedigree, a family tree, and bred carefully by experienced breeders.

When visiting your prospective breeder ask to see the KENNEL CLUB Registration ... of course it may be still with the KENNEL CLUB in progress and will be sent to you in due course ... simply, going to a regular breeder, who may also show at top level and has been a Beagle breeder for a long time, you can put your trust in them. They world also have a web site ... this is more confirmation they are genuine good breeders.

Usually a person who is serious about his dogs will ask you to wash your hands and take off your shoes as a precaution to bringing infection into the kennel. 'Parvo Virus' for example can be carried on shoes so again asking this is not only a good idea but also being safe against a dreaded disease..

Sometimes you are not allowed to handle the puppies and this is because of the fear of nasties being transferred to them ... no one is being rude, just guarded.

Seeing the Breeders set up will enlighten you, is it clean, are puppies happy, healthy active with clean eyes, no mess on them, also warm, no runny noses, chubby and with their Mum? Until they are 8/9 weeks old she will be in and out the puppy nest.

Mum must be on the premises and can be seen, Dad also if belonging to the breeder. If not a good photograph of him and his KENNEL CLUB Pedigree (it may of course be a copy), as he may have mated the bitch at the kennel Dad lives at.

Listen to the breeder she will tell you so much about the pups and the parents, it is a good idea to be wise and write down all the questions that might arise before your viewing.

Ask, ask, and ask, we breeders are only too pleased to air the details of their Beagles ... You can forget to ask sometimes as seeing the puppies for the first time is so exciting.

I never let folk come until the pups are 5 weeks old as it is unfair on Mum having strangers peering at the happy scene. That was my personal choice.

What about the papers and other items that will come with your chosen puppy?

There should be a contract, registrations, diet sheets, worming schedules, vaccination cards, information on toileting, exercise and training.

The contract needs to cover everything so when you go to collect your new 'furkid' you are armed with all the guides and advice from the breeder (they know best) not some-one you know on Facebook! !

Food, feeding guides, puppy play guides etc some folk ask for a piece of bedding so they are more settled at your home when they can smell and relate to their siblings.

Ideally if the owner can bring a hand towel then this can be placed in with the puppies at intervals, unwashed and then taken to their new home.

If this is your first visit you can make the date in your diary for collection when he/she is over 8 weeks of age (before that it is illegal in the UK). Usually it is best if you collect in a morning then you have many hours together to begin a relationship before bed time, puppy will then feel more secure.

When you are making your initial viewing appointment on the telephone, does the breeder sound welcoming, approachable and open to your questions?

Equally the breeder will be judging some of the conversation as to your suitability, they will ask questions as well, it is all for mutual benefits.
After 30 years plus of breeding I could tell on the telephone the suitability. If the first question is 'How much are they?' Then one of my pups is not for them. There are many answers I have heard and then declined a sale … as the Breeder I am the owner and I want the best possible home for each and every one of my puppies.

By this precaution I can say I have never had a puppy returned. I used to ask of their life style, work ethics, housing suitability, and is all the family in agreement? Also have they had a dog before, have they cats? If they work is there someone at home part of the day or will they hire a dog walker later or day care? If they go on holiday where will Beagle go? Do they live in a flat?

As an example, I had one elderly gentleman email me, then telephoned, interested in one of my pups. We had many a conversation between us and he said he would like to reserve a puppy paying by bank transfer (I had still not met him)

'No, please come and visit first' I had told him but the prospected client went on to explain he was in a Wheelchair. So, in my head I could see puppy being run over under a wheel! ! And who was going to exercise it later on ... I asked him he replied saying his wife world do everything ... ! !

Prior to this conversation he had told me his wife was in her 70's and did everything already! Shopping, cleaning, cooking nursing etc. In effect the puppy world be more work for his dear wife, and I felt I could not sell them a puppy for their sake and the pups. It world not have been fair on all of them.

Beagles are intelligent active dogs so how world that pan out when fully grown? I broke the news in an e-mail. I had a reply, slating me and later that day a begging one and then a phone call threatening me, saying he world report me to the KENNEL CLUB - err – why, what could they do? Not the way to endear oneself ... it was my choice to refuse a sale.

So, you want a puppy. Always be truthful and have insight, about, can you take on a puppy? Before handing over the money, be certain you will be able to cope with it when it grows into a dog!

You may say well I don't want to show nor breed, so the puppy for sale round the corner will do ... it won't, no health tests done, long term it may have temperament issues, or health issues, worm burden as a pup causing problems later.

I have even heard of cases where a sale takes place in a car park ... you may give over £350 and think you have a bargain ... however, it may cost you £££££'s more later on. You want to aim for the puppy you can afford and today £1000 plus is not unreal but you have the assurance he/she has had worming, registration, vaccinations, DNA tests and a host of other things, and from the word go has been socialised and nurtured by the breeder not raised in a cold stable or kennel.

Always be suspicious of a breeder who sells lots of breeds, you really need a Beagle Specialist, remember you are making an investment - if you don't have enough money then save until you do ... it will be worth the wait, the cheap poorly puppy will cost you more in the long run than a well-bred one.

Also you may have to travel or your puppy may come from another country these days the world is your Oyster, all my puppies I bred in Spain sold all over the world many going to UK mainly because of my reputation.

You may, of course buy an older Beagle or wish to take on one from a rescue, if this is the case consult 'Beagle Welfare' details of which are on their web site and also on Facebook.

Unfortunately, some folk are not prepared for a Beagle or their circumstances have changed thus moving the dog on ... of course, the dog may not have been trained and world have picked up a few odd habits ... you will be questioned about suitability as possibly the temperament is unknown. Here again a good breeder will either take the Beagle back or know someone suitable who is looking for one thus she can help. A bad breeder is one that suddenly does not answer the phone! ! ! !

Some other dog rescue charities such as 'Dog's Trust' will also have older dogs occasionally - it really depends on what you can take on and what your preference is.

Make an appointment first with the breeder of your choice, she will tell you if she has puppies now or older puppies or dogs and if not, she may recommend another breeder who has. Most good breeders will know each other from the Show Ring or just using their studs' dogs etc. It's akin to buying any animal, recommendations are earned so do not rush headlong into the purchase and regret it.

Most breeders, to keep a puppy for you will expect a deposit, then the puppy will be reserved, but should you decide not to go ahead with obtaining the dog, it is doubtful if your deposit will be returned. If there arises a problem with the puppy then the breeder has the right to withdraw from the sale and they will refund your deposit.

Chapter Two

Visiting your Chosen Breeder.

I remember those days when accepting visitors to see the puppies for a purchase. Most, if not all appointments are made over the telephone and one soon learns to judge someone's character just by the conversation. As I have previously said, 'I always say if the first question you ask is 'How Much?' then it immediately throws up a Red Flag! Because you have not read the advertisement or it figures too highly on the question ranking.

When you have made an appointment do not turn up with the entire family. I have had the prospective purchasers come with uninvited Granny, Grandad, Great Aunt, Cousins and family friends! ! ! I think one time 9 folk came as one to seek the puppy of their choice!

Some breeders will have puppies to see when you first make contact, there may be older puppies too, ones that a Show Breeder has kept just to see if one will shine out and be special for the ring.

Remember the Breeder has the first pick! A Beagle is a puppy up to 12 months of age so never walk away from the older ones either, they world have had their jabs, worming schedule and begun lead and toilet training.

So please tell the breeder it will either just be you and your partner and maybe a well-behaved child or two. Keep the appointment as a breeder's life is a busy one, also other folk may be going after your departure so if you cannot make it let her know.

When you arrive at the premises take a good look, is it a house or Kennels? Does it look clean and the garden well cared for? A dirty looking garden and rubbish etc strewn can be a red flag.

Never ever meet a breeder in a carpark or layby IT IS Puppy Farming. Be on time if you can, or phone them if delayed ... she may have a puppy viewing day and the next appointment will be waiting on the doorstep.

Before you set out, be certain to have your notepad with your questions in it, and don't think any questions are silly the breeder world have heard them all.

You may have come a long way by car and you must expect to travel some distance as the nearest good breeder may not be down the road. So, after taking off your shoes and washing your hands with soap provided (protection for the puppies) as infection can be brought in (Parvo Virus is one).

Choose a breeder who has done the DNA swab test for known Beagle diseases MLS, NCCD, FV11 and Lafora. All breeds of dogs are likely to have genetic faults carried through the line. Unless the parentage is negative then the Bitch and the Stud Dog used for a litter will be used so puppies are not affected.

You have every right to see the results if you are making a purchase and the Breeder will be happy to assist you. It does not mean your Puppy will be exempt from other genetic faults i.e. Cherry Eye is a good example. All these can be viewed on WWW. BeagleHealth on a PC if you are unfamiliar with the above.

An Assured Breeder will of course have done these swabs and a good breeder will have anyway, as it is no good leaving it to chance and producing a litter not suitable for showing or rearing.

Ask to see any paperwork, i.e. Registrations (if they are back from the KENNEL CLUB). The CONTRACT, this is important, you are buying, and they are selling, so I cannot emphasise enough the need for both of you to have a signed the contract. This will state the terms of the sale which, having read it you need to sign.

It world have had in the document worming schedule, vaccinations, feeding chart, endorsements (on the KENNEL CLUB reg) explained monies paid and all things appertaining to the puppy. There may also be a 4 or 5 Generation Pedigree, and this is where the history of the breeding line is.

I also gave documents on feeding, exercise, poisons, with lots of tips regarding toileting and training by reward. I will detail these in the next Chapter.

So now you see the litter and Mum is there. She may be in and out to see her pups and at five weeks may come and greet you or be in the garden doing her toileting. Most bitches will be possessive or will not like strangers so the breeder may have taken her away from the whelping area whilst you take a look at the pups.

I always used tiny material collars to identify each puppy. If I had 2 I wanted to keep for myself or maybe the breeder has sold one, these may be in another pen or whelping box so you only get to see the ones available, be they bitch pups or males.

This is totally up to the breeder but from the buyer's point of view it can be very confusing looking at 8/9 or 13 pups and deciding which one??? It's like finding an edge piece of a 5000 jigsaw puzzle! The less you need to see and the easier the choice will be.

Obviously after making your decision the other puppies will be returned and Mum can come and meet you so you can see her. She may be very proud to show you her pups but do not spend too much time with her as her babies need her.

All our mums were happy to see folk but only after 5 weeks as I feel it's not fair on her being subjected to strangers. If the Stud dog resides there to, go and see him ... see if he is friendly as well and, of course he should be a handsome Beagle with good bone, plenty of substance and quality.

Again, the bitch must be feminine with good quality looks. Ask to see the health test results they will be on the registrations as endorsements, if any. This endorsement means the breeder has asked the KENNEL CLUB to place a 'stop' on the data and registration to say the puppy cannot be bred from UNLESS the endorsement is lifted at a later stage by the breeder writing to the KENNEL CLUB on your behalf. There may be a fee for such like, it is up to the Breeder.

Even if you say well, we don't want to breed ... down the line or if the pup is sold on ... it could happen, if so without releasing the endorsement there can be no registration on the new pups!

I think half to an hour is plenty at the breeders remember they are busy people. Be courteous, and if there is someone else coming to view make it positive.

When we lived in Spain one couple came from London by car to choose their second Bizarte Beagle and then drove back thousands of miles ... then if you travel in a Porsche Carrera so world I!

Chapter Three

Choosing Your Puppy -

Male or Female???? That is the question.

So, you have arrived, following a detailed telephone conservation about what you are seeking, and confirming the breeder has what you are looking for.

Now you can see your puppy ... there may be a choice of two or three or even just the one as others may have already been chosen or the breeder will specify that there is one suitable and has chosen it for you.

I personally like to choose myself but again each breeder is different. Hopefully you have remembered your question book and now is the time to ask. The puppies should look clean, full tummies, smell lovely and the pen and bedding clean, with access to water and heated lamp or hot plate for pups. Also, if Mum is with them is she allowed to go in and out at her leisure?

Basically, you should be seeing a happy scene ... clear bright eyes, no snotty noses and if they are awake, playful and curious and maybe there are some safe toys already in the nest. Do not pick the one that comes to you, bites you or hides in the corner just for those reasons. You must look at the Breed Standard again on the KENNEL CLUB site or

Google it. You want the puppy that is chunky, with a full tummy, a happy outgoing attitude, not whining or looking disinterested.

Again, some breeders will let you hold ... but I preferred to hold the puppy for the client to see (if you break it you pay for it!) they will then talk you through each one, if there is a choice. NOW! are you going for a male or female? Dilemma, me thinks. I have been asked hundreds of time what is the difference in temperament?

Well I can say from experience a Bitch Puppy is loving just as playful as a male and needing the same requirements.

You don't want to breed so you may want to spay at around 2 years old ... . . A Male pup is adventurous and playful and has a more wanderlust brain and will use it later on to go on an adventure if not trained to recall. If you think logically this is because the Bitch whelps and nurtures her puppies while the male provides the fertility and is a hunter by nature of the Breed.

Again you may wish to castrate later and the best time is as the dog nears two years old, or after when all the growing is done. Hormones such as oestrogen and testosterone are required for good development of bone density and muscle also brain cells so it is never a good idea to do these things early if at all ... popular belief has it they will calm down and be more obedient in nature but if the Beagle is operated on around year two this moment occurs naturally … thus a lot of folk think its down to the neutering … not totally.

The bitch puppy will come into season at some point, not necessarily at 6 months it is just a guesstimate. One bitch I owned had her first season at two years old exactly on her birthday! Some may be at four months or others at twelve months there is no right or wrong way. The boys have their testosterone and it's all down now to your training routine.

I have seen over the years many folk buying pants and towels for their bitch … really this is not necessary as she will keep herself clean it will not be like a Chain Saw Massacre … more likely to be spot of blood which changes to brown for a week or so.

The season lasts 21 days normally in an adult bitch but as a pup it may well be shorter and lighter. Her mating hormones rise around nine to thirteen days and her last week is when she is ready in and around that time for mating by the male. You will just have to keep her in your garden for exercise or lead walk her in quiet places away from other dogs.

A Male dog can smell a bitch in season from a long way away and could be knocking at your door or joining you on your walk, so the local park is not the best place.

I used to walk in the countryside and avoid other dogs but I remember one time a Labrador followed us and I had to act swiftly shooing him away. There is a book I can recommend called 'Book of the Bitch' and in this you will find some very informative paragraphs on this subject. It was my Bible when I first began Breeding but a very useful book for general information.

Most of my male customers world choose a Male (it's a man thing!) whilst Ladies prefer the female. Sometimes you may go with one sex in mind and completely change if there is a choice! Know the Standards of The Breed ... this can be found on the KENNEL CLUB web site

Chapter Four

So... questions to ask ... ...

1/ *Is there a Contract?*

You and the Breeder are making a transaction of sale so a contract will define what you are buying, all the details of the puppy and the Breeders terms. On it will be your details, the Breeders name, and details of the puppy and state the terms and conditions regarding return of the puppy, monies at any stage.

I always wrote that I must be informed first if they cannot continue owning the puppy. Also, Free 14 day pet insurance from the Breeder through an Insurance company so you are insured from word go on collection.

I used Pet Plan and found them really good. Your puppy is then covered for terms in the Insurance pack and they will get in touch if you wish to Insure through them after the 14 day period.

You must be able to see the mother with her puppies when you go to view ... . if you cannot then it's a Red Flag warning ... step away from the puppy pen!

2/ *The Puppy pack?*

This is made up by the Breeder and should include ...

Food for the puppy what it is eating now … remember there are going to be many changes for him/her so continuing with the same brand or at a later stage a gradual changeover if required can be made.

In the pack there should be: Diet sheets of when and how much food, also extra's … I fed Weetabix. Farley's Rusks daily with Goat's Milk or Lactose Free Milk. Puppies do not tolerate Lactose which is in cow's milk as milk makes Mucus … but the Goat's is nutritious and also yoghurt's too.

I also gave calcium tablets; these can be found in large pet stores. Calcium is needed for good bone development and density … incidentally foals also need it and as I have bred a few, know this to be true.

I have seen tins of Puppy Milk full of Nutrients and this is good also. White fish such as Coley can be steamed and fed with brown Rice. As a Supper dish scrambled egg and raw beef mince also bone building and enjoyable.

I used to feed 4 times a day up to 3 months then 3 times a day and still do. Little and often is kinder to a puppy's belly and very large rotund bellies can cause explosive Diarrhoea. Chews under careful eye and only those for a puppy are great for boredom relief and Kong's filled with Shipham's Paste, cream cheese or Peanut butter.

I found baby toys from Mothercare good as they were safe for a baby. Your puppy will have baby teeth, and these will drop out at about 12-16 weeks. You do not want to damage the root beds whilst forming, so plenty of soft toys and no tugs of war games!

You can also feed a pro-biotic in the food and Pro Plan make special powders available in large Pet stores. It is important to feed him in his playpen especially if you have children, it should be a calm time and let him enjoy the food. A puppy pad can be in place ready for business of the day.

3/ *Now let's discuss the other end!*

Your puppy will tinkle all through the day a male puppy will squat like the female for some months until he finds balancing on one leg!

Poops will arrive after eating and a little play or skip the play and whoops! Here it comes. The puppy may whine and turn in circles concentrating on the matter in hand, it could go behind your telly, on your favourite knitting pattern or if you have been soft, on your bed! ! !

If you have some newspaper put down a thick pad and then a puppy pad on top, place puppy on it; So, in every room your puppy is in, you will be prepared. Maybe have a play or puppy pen or utility room with a gate on so puppy can eat in there and do his business! This is the easiest way. Then he will learn this is where he can relax and abide by the rules of the house.

DO NOT SCOLD puppy if there are mistakes or accidents it is totally natural to relieve themselves, it is up to you where!

Physically they cannot control the musculature of the bladder or bowels when young. Keep wet wipes handy these are going to be a godsend when travelling in the car or walkies etc.! !

Fox poo is a favourite perfume of the young hound and he/she can find the smelliest dead fish on the Beach ... great when you are all in an enclosed area or the car on the way home .

4/ Dew Claws

Dew claws, are they still attached, or have they been removed? Important to know as these hanging nails can cause problems later to some dogs. though they can be left on. I removed all mine and my dogs never had back dew claws! I removed them at 2/3 days with the correct tools, after that it is too late as the nervous system may have kicked in.

5/ Diet

Ask what to feed, what the breeder is giving and

when, quantity and timings. I gave my new owners the food puppy is on now, so the same can be fed for as long as it is required. (Sorry, all this is worth repeating) I found 4 meals a day of 75gm kibble or a different choice say a cereal or cooked fish.

As I said raw beef mince goes down well and will provide protein. Feeding is an art form and judging the tummy and poops state will become regular to you. You can assess the health of your Beagle by its eating and pooping!

As your Beagle grows, it can be changed onto a junior feed if well covered there is nothing worse than a skinny Beagle. Stand back and access him sideways on ... and from above , does he/she have shape, well stacked ribs and is healthy in coat, eyes shiny and nose freezing, and carries his tail gaily?

Is he/she happy to see his food coming? Be careful here for if you begin changing every meal, he/she will look for your dinner! ! ! I feed leftover veg, cooked meats say from a Roast dinner as a separate meal ... you can, of course, go RAW and I have also done this but feeding so many Beagles each meal became like an abattoir and as I enjoy knitting my hands were rather smelly!

There are many really good brands of Kibble some really high in meats and protein obviously they are more expensive, but they love it and it can make the stools easier to pick up and dispose of ... incidentally feed chicken wings RAW ... NEVER COOKED. They can be given as a treat daily. These give calcium and clean the teeth and are enjoyed with gusto.

6/ *Vaccinations and Microchip*

Your puppy will have started his vaccinations at the Breeders. She will have a card with the type used and date administered by the vets.

If you are collecting him at 8/9 weeks and are local to the same vet you can take your Puppy back to him to continue the vaccination course. If outside that area your vet may prefer a different brand and start again . It really is the vet's choice.

Until those vaccinations are completed and the vet tells you when he/she is free to go outside, he/she must stay in the house. Cats, rats and foxes carry diseases dangerous to puppies so be aware these creatures may well come in your garden. Also people visiting your home may carry similar on their shoes so if your puppy is around the house ask them to remove their footwear as a precaution.

The puppy may have been chipped by the vet at the same time as vaccination. I am a fully trained Microchip implanter so I did all my own puppies prior to leaving for their new homes and registered the number with the Data base at the KENNEL CLUB. It is the law that all puppies/dogs must be chipped.

7/ Toilet Training

Where does one start? So as puppies cannot physically control their bladder or bowels when young I always use pads from the local pet shop or buy in Bulk on line. You eventually move the pad nearer the door and can then put puppy in the garden, when the vaccinations are finished, for it to toilet.

Tell the puppy he/she is good in a really soft voice and stroke him after he/she checks out on the pad ... he/she will soon learn this is the correct place to go. Don't become obsessed with toileting it will happen eventually, there is no point getting in a stew he/she is a baby therefore expect anything. Don't let it become all important ... it is not ... just clean up and continue...

8/ Sleeping?

Your Puppy and you!

The important word for you is SLEEP. So, it's very like having a new-born. Sleep deprivation can occur for a few days or not ... there is no 'on/off' switch. Puppy will have naps during the day, he or she, needs this to relax and feel safe.

You need a crate or puppy's own space in a warm place away from children or noise. This will be known as

Puppy's Place. This should be a safe haven with a few cuddly toys , a pad, water, a play pen is ideal and it sets you free to go shopping, house work, or other for an hour or so. Leave a radio or television on if you have to pop out for an hour.

My Beagle's NEVER go in the bedrooms ... it is your space and you will need it to sleep without interruption.

Puppies can pee on bedding, play and generally misbehave on beds and jumping down or falling can damage joints. And they will play up (howl) if you change your mind and refuse them to go upstairs or your sleeping quarters. START as you mean to go on.

A friend of mine slept with 5 dogs on her bed with her husband. . they always looked haggard and had sleep deprivation ... and don't say just this once! ! ! A beagle will be tenacious, and you will give in to its demands. You could leave a radio on low or have a ticking clock near his pen ... I always turn lights out. He/she is not going to read!

Chapter Five

Ask about exercise?

Nothing until the Vaccinations are complete remember. And once clear it should be limited. It really is a case of in the garden at the beginning, recommendation for puppies is 5 mins per month of age on hard ground, i.e. Tarmac or pavements.

The young puppy's bones are soft and growing from the joints that's why they are knuckle shape. If there is over exercise these joints can become more inflamed and over grow into long thin bone. so softly softly at first .

Then you can gradually build up to a proper walk later when puppy is 6 months or so. Also do not let him jump off furniture, stairs or steps. Again, the joints can be aggravated. Cherish him in his early days and you will reap rewards.

Travel Home on the pickup day!

Get a small crate or carrier and have a pad in and carry towels, kitchen roll and a safe soft toy. Don't be tempted to have the pup on your lap, its very likely he/she will be sick with the motion and you will be covered. If you have told the Breeder time of collection keep to it as she may well have not fed puppy or only a tiny bit so that he/she will hopefully not sick it up.

Okay, you may say it is over an hour away. I have travelled puppies 4 hours away and they are in the back of the car in a crate with the above ... most of the time they sleep and we never stop for toileting as your pup may try to escape and this could be very dangerous if on a layby or somewhere similar.

Chapter Six

Other pets

What about if you have a cat, or you already have a dog or another Beagle? If the cat is not a vicious type then you can introduce him gradually ... you are the only one who will know the cat and what he/she may do. I do know that someone's puppy had a very nasty eye injury from a cat's claw so be aware.

If an ear flap is scratched it will bleed profusely. The puppy will not realise it is a Cat, but a play friend and take liberties. You will have to introduce them gradually, as some cats will not adjust to a new stranger in their territory.

I have several owners that have cats and still have Beagles. But my Pack at home world always see them off, should they have entered the garden or on a roof.

When you introduce a puppy into the home with another dog you will have to be in gradual steps. The puppy will not be able to play rough and tumble as he/she could be injured, sometimes the older dog might object to being harassed by the puppy and respond by nipping him. I have found females easier to bond a friendship with a new puppy, she may well put him in his place but will have a nurturing side.

Boy to boy then you may have problems with hierarchy and more so later when Testosterone is rising. I have never encountered a problem as long as you take steps to introduce them slowly and supervised - never leave them together in a small area, like a crate. Beagles are quite accommodating but remember the well-bred Beagle will hold its temperament which I talked about earlier. A mixed Beagle may carry traits of other Breeds and not be so accommodating!

Also if you decide to buy 2 puppies together prepare for mayhem and getting attention for training will be very hard. A one to one is always the way forward in bonding with yourself.

Holidays and high days.

Personally, I do not like Commercial Kennels. I do have experience of them, and it was not good. I much prefer to use a house and pet sitter for holidays or to another Beagle owner who has one or two and are happy to board yours in their home. Your breeder may have him short term and, at the time of writing expect to pay around £15 per day

You can then enjoy yourself not worrying about 'your precious baby'! It's a good idea to have your Beagle and the house sitter or pet boarder to meet up and see how everybody gets on before committing yourself. You will have peace of mind knowing that your 'furkid' is also having a holiday.. Especially if your Beagle is one of the family then there are many hotels, holiday homes and the like who will allow your pet to holiday with you. You may even decide to travel abroad, and it is not difficult to get a Pet Passport, also injections and health tests to allow you to travel in a car together to a holiday destination.

As well as going away there may be days when you are working or not available at home then go to a Doggy Day Care have a look. This may suit your Beagle short term and some even board overnight too! Visit them and look, they should be happy to show you round and explain how it works. Far better to get these things sorted for the future and some may also have Puppy classes, great for socialisation.

Talking of which it is advisable to get your puppy well socialised by meeting children other dogs, streets with traffic, shops and trains. (I used to have my neighbours' children visit the dogs often). I have also seen mine on Canal and sailing boats obviously wearing correct harness for safety. The more he/she sees and gets used to mentally, the more he/she will be easier to train and handle.

Your Children

Your children may come to the breeders to see the puppies and great excitement will occur ... I have had children mentally challenged who after having a Beagle at home changed and become more outgoing because of the bond between themselves and the dog. One little boy was deaf and very shy, but when he came a second time it was lovely to see him sitting with his arm draped around the puppy next to him.

Some children may be anxious especially if they have had a nasty experience with dogs. They need time for adjustment, so if the breeder has lots and lots of Beagles running around, which can be daunting as Beagles are nosy by nature. They may jump up and frighten the child. Inform the breeder when you make the appointment for viewing or collection, who is coming. They will then be prepared and can be ready to make sure the event is calm. When you have your puppy finally at home, show your children how to pet their new friend. Certainly not to lift it up or scream at the bundle of fur ... explain the boundaries.

Usually the breeder will acknowledge your children's attitude and help you in how the child or children approach having a puppy, they must be taught in not pulling the tail, pinching nor feeding your furkid. You must lay down the rules and then all the family can enjoy the Beagle to the full ... as he/she is an approachable chap and well-bred Beagles are non-aggressive and make great family dogs, treated properly.

Chapter
Seven

Payment ! ! ! !

A deposit will be required, as mentioned for your chosen one and a receipt given. That will also be on the Contract and this you will obtain at collection. The breeder will telephone the Insurance and issue you with a Voucher to cover your puppy as explained previously, for 14 days.

If you are going to pay the remainder of the purchase by Cheque then send it in the post so it can be banked prior to collection, in other words it must have cleared first! Cash is Key although Credit cards can be a way of paying providing the breeder has the facilities to accept them. Understand the Contract before you sign it and the breeder will sign to say you have read it and agreed it.

Always get support from your breeder, if you have any concerns ring them and ask. Its far better to use expert knowledge than asking a question or searching the problem on social media first! They will be more than happy to advise … it's your first port of call.

Chapter Eight

He/she's Home ! whoop whoop ...

YOU are Officially a Beagle Owner!

So you have collected your furkid and have made it home ... hopefully you have collected it in the morning so you have the rest of the day before nightfall to get to know each other and he/she the new surroundings.

Let him have a cool drink and leg stretch with his toys before any feeding. Travelling can dehydrate him so plenty of liquids and he/she will obviously need to toilet so show him where and his special chill space. You should have this ready and then there are no rush decisions ... preparation is key.

You world have discussed and worked out where his space is going to be ... hopefully ... a utility room if its ambient or has a radiator. A space under the stairs or kitchen if it is large. Your new friend will need heating, lighting and a soft fleece like 'Vetbed,' easily washable and hygienic. We never use anything else other than a soft snuggly blanket so Puppy can scrape and make a nest with it.

You will need a ticking clock or low radio, water bowl (get one that cannot be tipped over) also puppy proof toys and make sure chewable toys are safe and that they cannot pull out the eyes or squeakers. Let him relax around the room and he/she may curl up and sleep as travel can be very tiring ... pop him in his bed and carry on with your routine.

When he/she wakes let puppy relieve himself on the pad in the pen, offer the new friend their food it does not matter about the time you will get into a routine when you start out tomorrow. After furkid has enjoyed his food you have prepared then he/she may poop ... then it's out of the pen for play, cuddles and getting to know each other ... have his name ready and call him he/she will come and reward him with play and cuddles.

When the evening comes do not let him get over tired or over excited keep everybody calm and then when you are going to bed get him ready for that too! A light supper for him/her like Farley's rusk or Weetabix with Lactose free milk or Goat's milk. Then he/she will want to relieve themselves either on waking prior to supper or after.

He/she may have fallen asleep on your lap, place him in his 'safe' place and have water, his toys and something warm ready for the new member of the family. Beagles like all puppies will want to tiddle frequently they cannot hold on ... both sexes will squat. Remember poops will come after food. Do not get obsessed with toileting just clean up and its all normal.

Kitchen rolls and wet wipes are invaluable for puppy cleaning and smell lovely too. If you have children try and explain he/she is a baby dog and not to punish him they will get it eventually. At first children might be excited about it but will be bored of the sameness real soon.
Maybe you have taken time off from your job to settle your new puppy into a routine. I must say puppy ownership is like having a baby, he/she needs you 24/7. He/she needs feeding, toileting, training, love, warmth they will depend on it.

So, if you work normally part-time then you can begin your routine, hopefully there are other family members there when you are not. (I never sell to full time workers it's not fair on the dog or yourselves and family). He/she cannot be left alone as a puppy or as a grown dog. He/she will become very destructive and bored and probably almost untrainable with no routine to follow.

If you work shifts and another member is at home then they have to be a surrogate mother! Some folk have dog walkers when he/she is older BUT you must still be home part of the day, as suggested day care maybe better later on but only as a temporary place, not every day ... what's the point in having a dog? A Beagle is part of your family he/she enjoys people and feels the love. The more you put in the more you will get out it's a two-way street.

Routine now will all revolve around your Beagle puppy. Hopefully, you will have had a good night and are ready for your day ahead. Change his pad if soiled which is more than likely ... and prepare his breakfast a good quality puppy food from the breeder.

Then he/she may use his pad and then he/she needs to come out of the pen to get accustomed to his surroundings. Make sure cables, telephone wires, TV remotes and any plug sockets air fresheners are removed and placed out of reach. Also your Jimmy Choos, handbags, school books and pens, Beagles have no Boundaries and are not fussy!

I had a letter chewed having been delivered through the door. Inside was a cheque for £300 luckily, I managed to retrieve bits and sellotaped it back together and LLOYDS bank accepted it.

Now is the time when you need to get a routine going. Animals thrive on routine. So, you have 4 meals a day going on (until around 6 months) then you can decrease times but not the quantity. You must feed according to activity. He/she needs protein and carbs, stand away from them does he/she look a chubba wubba or are their ribs well sprung, Look from above does he/she have a bulging tummy, or just gently rounded.

No beagle looks good skinny so make sure all his meals are nutritious and eaten up if he/she leaves any food pick the bowl up and discard. Make sure you wash all his bowls in hot soapy water. He/she will play now with their toys. Your interaction also the children … must be gentle and also with firm commands, if you are calling him to you or telling him No. Never strike your puppy he/she will never forget so enjoy these early days. If it is cold, he/she needs warmth, cuddles and he/she will get to know your voice.

When he/she comes to you give it a favourite toy as a reward. Toys can be a simple plastic bottle lid taken off, dry flannel, soft toys, (I repeat myself by saying - check the eyes cannot be pulled out) tie a knot in a mans sock great for shaking and tossing. You can go to a car boot sales or baby stores, supermarket and get toys for baby. If they are used check everything well and wash, and don't forget those tiny teeth can pull out stuffing in seconds.

You can buy the most expensive dog toys and he/she will still prefer that old sock! Children can sit on the floor at this age and get involved gently no holding up in the air or tug of wars. Children should be supervised, and you can interact as a family. He/she will love you all.

I get a lot of questions about Biting and see these posts regularly on Social Media. All puppies will use their teeth it is akin to the hand. So provide plenty of toys especially for your pet to chew on. He/she has Baby teeth and his urge to teeth will be strong. His next set of Adult teeth come at about 12-16 weeks. You may be lucky and find them about the play area before the Tooth Fairy!

What is a good idea in the evening or afternoon when you are seated and relaxing, place puppy on your lap and with clean fingers place in his mouth along the tooth line and massage. He/she will retract probably but will in time allow it a little.

This has always worked for me as he/she will now associate your fingers as not tasty and he/she will be less interested in biting.

You will have to make your children understand he/she is not being aggressive just mouthing on them a way of playing. It's like a pony in respect of handling them as they know no different … you can later use your voice to retract from rough play.

When in the litter nest and playing with siblings it is what they do, and some will squeal when nipped too hard. Make sure his toys are his siblings to play with.

In time he/she will respect you and this stage will be over. Importantly if he/she has something in their mouth he/she is not supposed to have, do not yank it out. Instead get something he/she likes and swap, get his attention and trade his item for yours never attempt to take it off of him with no reward. It is like a treasure and he/she needs to be distracted to give it up. The above also applies when he/she is much older. If he/she steals something then exchange is the way forward. Do not let your children get involved ... see to it quickly and calmly.

Exercise is very limited for good reason in the early weeks ... once the vaccinations are over and the time lapse for cover then he/she can go out and about. I repeat the recommended - 5 mins per month of age on hard services no more but overdo the exercise and his joints will suffer. Your Furkid can play happily in the garden on grass as it is soft and there is a little give in the ground. Tarmac, pavements and concrete have no bounce so the impact on young bones especially the joints, where growth plates are inflamed already, will impact his bone formation.

You want your new friend to have short dense bone structure and with too much exercise you may end up with long thin bones or a bone malformation such as Carpal Valgus where the front legs are at 10 to 2 from the front view, bit like a seal.

If you have to go out and you need not be confined to the house, place puppy in his pen leave the television or radio on low and make sure there are toys, water of course and a snuggly bed. Again, I repeat as it is important - do not go out all day but an hour or so is fine. He/she will probably sleep between playing. I good idea is to fill a Puppy Kong with cream cheese or crab paste, he/she will be happy for ages.

I have known folk buy two puppies at the same time, but I think it is much easier if you do not, as attention will not be on yourself but always on the sibling. If you already have another Beagle or dog then still pop puppy in the pen. Sometimes puppies can annoy the older dog and you don't want a fight to hurt the puppy. Two Beagle puppies together can cause mayhem, so you are their provider and they know it, together you are an item.

Safety for your pet is paramount as a Kamikaze puppy has no idea that an electric cable can kill him. I was ironing once and unbeknown to me under the ironing board one of my older puppies was chewing through the lead. 'BANG' and a yelp! as the dog shot into the conservatory and then the garden. Thankfully the little friend was fine and only suffered the instant shock ... so it can happen! Eventually it went on to win many rosettes ... had they been a much younger puppy, things may have been very different!

Vets ... ...

Your trips and Relationship.

Your vet is a qualified general practitioner of pets, cats, dogs, hamsters and other types of animals. He/she is not a Beagle Specialist. BUT they are your first port of call should you suspect or see puppy is not well.

Occasionally your puppy will have perhaps Diarrhoea or sickness. Rich food or a change in diet even water may upset his digestive system … so if the stools have blood in, mucous and are really smelly and he/she is lethargic, not interested in food then seek your vet as soon as possible

Puppies can be treated quickly but can also go downhill at the same speed. Often dehydration will cause listlessness and a very sick puppy is harder to treat. He/she may have worms, hopefully not and has had the full schedule of that treatment. So they should be wormed from word go and throughout. At the breeders and then on leaving following the treatment as on the worming plan.

Make sure you can see the vet on the same day, if you have a good relationship with your vet they may say come down now. I never had to wait, even in Spain, I was always seen rapidly. It may be a case of he/she has picked up a bug, swallowed something not right so by talking with your vet you can get the right treatment.

The puppy's temperature will show if he/she has any bugs or bacteria, then anti-biotics can be started as soon as possible. Also, treatment for the gut flora. Interestingly Pro Plan sell sachets of Pro-biotin good for upset tummies and these you can put in puppy's food ... obviously quantity is per recommendation on the sachet information.

I feed Goats milk and Yoghurt and again good flora can help see him through the intestinal problem. The yoghurt I feed daily and have found it to be very beneficial in my Beagles. Chicken cooked with rice is good and they love it. . don't wash all the starch out of the rice as this helps bind the stools.

You may, of course, prefer home prepared meals with meat and vegetables, or feeding Raw ... there are many social sites on it that may help you. I did feed Raw once but, as I said previously my kitchen resembled an abattoir. My vet said bacteria could get into the digestive system more readily ... so if you only have one or two Beagles you can buy quantities from your Butchers. But, I world say the ready prepared raw in say 'Pets At Home' is a great way to feed uncooked.

Some of the Kibbles are excellent and I found Burn's, Canigan and Wolfheart are really good, they will be much more expensive than run of the mill supermarket feeds but will be the best food high in proteins.

Feeding does seem to be the highest form of confusion with Beagles. There is a mountain of different feeds to choose from and feeding is an art form in as much as to look at your Beagle judgmentally. Does he/she look healthy? With a shiny coat, bright eyes, tail carried gaily, full of life ... are his ribs well sprung covered but not bloated with fat. Is your puppy a jolly happy chap that eats up and may look for more? You develop an 'eye' for his shape ... don't let him get obese ... it's harder to get weight off than on. Feed according to age, exercise and condition.

Beagles will when healthy devour almost anything, your own socks, plastic, empty food containers, I could go on so always be alert when out and about as folk leave all kinds of rubbish which your Beagle may enjoy BUT, cause you a lot of Money at the vets.

Also other poisonous foods such as grapes, onions, mushrooms and chocolate in quantity will mean a trip to the vets all of these can be fatal .... read all about it at The KENNEL CLUB of GB on your PC.

Let's talk about colours ... .

These are the standard colours. Tricolour, as above Black, Tan and White ... in time the black may fade, and she world be as she is becoming a, 'Faded tri'. At birth Beagles are born Black and White, the Tan will develop over the next weeks.

The marking can clearly be seen at birth, if she was a Lemon Beagle when born she world have been almost white also it is more difficult to see the markings.

BeagleTypes ... ...

Well as a Judge ... Type is everything...

If you have a pig that looks like a llama then it's not a pig.! ! !

The Beagle standard type is what you should be seeking. As I say 'Type is everything' ... by this I mean good short cannon bones, knee and hock definition when a puppy, ear flaps not set high, tail set high and carried, strong back, snout in balance on the head, nose strong, well sprung ribs and stocky feet.

He or she should resemble the Breed Standard as close as possible and obviously your puppy will take on the genetic genes from the line of dad, mum, grandparents and so on. Oh! I hear you say, I don't want a show dog just a pet. It should still be of the same quality and will fare well because of it.

Long spindly cannon bones, tails sent low like the ears, small flaps, long nose these are not the good traits so could well mean there has been a
mating somewhere in the line that may well have been a mongrel! !

Bizarte Harry at 10 weeks

So once we are going out and about your puppy should see his world. . cars, trains, people, children playing, in other words daily life. The earlier he/she is introduced to noise and happenings the better they will adjust.

Fireworks are noisy and can be frightening with flashing lights. I am not suggesting your Beagle should be at a display for one moment but when at home you must show no fear as this will rub off onto your dog.

When we lived in Spain, they have endless firework fiesta's and all our beagles became 'de sensitized' in the end and were not frightened, although were not outside but in the house.

It is true that Beagles will feel your tension or apprehension and feed off of that. Don't make a fuss just behave normally turn the television or radio up, have a warm cosy place to snuggle with you ... you can also buy vests called Thundershirts . . these look like Babygro's and hold your Beagle as if in a snuggle so he/she feels safe.

I used mine after any operation on the dog and found them invaluable. I have never used a CONE, the thing that is like a lampshade and fits around their head, I do not support their use. I have seen miserable looking Beagle wearing the Cone of Shame and I see depression in their eyes ... also it is an add on financially at the vets.

I do not recommend Car Boot Sales either. The amount of times I have seen folk dragging their pooch around people's legs ... let's face it that is all a dog gets to see. Leave him at home because your Beagle will not enjoy it.

CAR journeys ... ...

Yes its true, he/she will be sick! So how to avoid and what you will need. Do not feed your Beagle if you are going in the car with him because he/she will give it back to you once travelling!

If you are heading out in the morning no breakfast, only of course his water. You need about 5 hours before the journey with no food and that includes tit bits. Now if you are going in the car a.m., the night before a light supper say chicken and rice and add Ginger grated to the meal or Ginger biscuits crumbled, great for nausea.
You can, of course take your puppy in a crate at the rear of the car for short journey's say 10-15 mins and build the times up so your Beagle will get accustomed to the car trips. Always feed on your return.

Chapter Nine

Out and About ... ...

In general puppies should be outgoing and curious. If you decide to go out before vaccinations then you must carry them as I said he/she will not be protected.

Do not let your children pick him up they could drop him accidentally and break a bone ... he/she is your baby after all!

Let your new friend see the cars, the noise also other folk but do not let other dogs sniff him in greeting which could a) Pass germs over ... b) turn aggressive.

Always, always, be aware of other dogs no matter how sweet their owner will say... things can turn nasty in a nano second and your puppy will not be able to defend itself!

So now puppy is older, and you have been practising your re-call at Rincraft training classes, (look at the KENNEL CLUB website for one near you). In the garden use a long line attached to a harness not the neck! Then off the lead and reward every time he/she comes to you ... 'Aniseed Show Bait' is best but he/she loves cubed cheddar, cocktail sausages or even a tube of Primula, do not use his Kibble as he/she already has this and it world be boring.

Then when you feel optimistic go to an enclosed park but be sure there will be no aggressive dogs around. A Beagle meet up pre - arranged is a good choice and he/she will be among his own. You can find these on the Social Media sites so take a look.

You can of course take a drive into the countryside and find a peaceful walk away from traffic, take your treats in a Bum Bag, and a whistle or bell. You can buy whistles in good pet shops. If you have done the groundwork at home he/she will come back readily for his treat. Make the whole enjoyable and return unfazed ready for a peaceful afternoon zzzzzzzzz.

Oh Beagle has gone? ? ?

Yes, its true it does happen ... here's what to do. (*You will find stories of my true events further into this book!)*

Do not panic ... keep calm. So, say you have parked in a carpark and walked from there. He/she will either chase wildlife (mine love a Deer) Pheasants and Rabbits or even a Fox! He/she will eventually give up having lost the prey and his sense of smell is amazingly strong and will find his own scent and follow it back hopefully to where you were.

Now this may take time ... be prepared stay where you are and use your whistle periodically. If you can hear he/her then call. Your new friend may be screeching (baying or singing) and that means it is on the scent, stop whistling they will not return until he/she has given up or is worn out.

If a lot of time has passed then go back and check the car park he/she may well go there but do not go home or leave the place from where he/she ran off.

Bizarte Never Been Kissed aka Nelli Bean

It is sometimes a good idea to place an old dirty sweatshirt of yours or part of his smelly bedding at the tyre of your car he/she will know and stay there should he/she come back. Now if he/she stay's out you will have to get help from friends and family but do not leave the area.

There are Beagles that have gone off and you may need a Beagle wearing a tracker for their to help.

Regarding getting a Tracker that is worn on the collar of the dog this is a great idea and you can see where he/she is on your mobile.

In all these years I have had all of the above and will recount these happenings for you which will guide your Beagle ownership. There is no Magic Wand I am sorry to say, it goes with the Scent Hound----- The Beagle. If you are truly worried then only let him free in an enclosed area and use a long line (horses lung line for example) when going out and about.

Separation Anxiety … … … … …

If you work full time then really it is not logical to have a dog, any dog. He/she will need you like a baby needs its mother … . . ok for an hour or so if you need shopping etc. but a day is a day too long!

I never sell any puppy or older Beagle to folk that will leave it. If you or your partner work from home then fine and I have owners that do.

Your family must all want the puppy and know what the criteria is for the looking after it, as it means as a new-born it is demanding! You cannot possibly expect harmony in the camp if the dog is left in solitary.

You may say well a neighbour pops in, the furkid has toys, and will be in a play pen with the television on ... NO, NO it does not work. You will either come home to a letter from your neighbours about the howling ... the dog has destroyed everything in the pen including the pen and/or he/she has got out and destroyed the house ... peed everywhere - and the other, Also eaten god only knows what?

If you work shift's or part-time or part of a week then let your furkid go to day care where he/she can mix with others like them self.

Okay, you must budget it in but you will find a well-adjusted Beagle makes it all so worthwhile. Doggy day care services are everywhere, and you can find them in Yellow Pages and no doubt Google.

When your Beagle is older you may prefer a Dog Walker it is trial and error. The odd occasions I used them was when I was away filming or for other reasons when I was not available. Also, I had a dear friend who has two Beagles herself that world come and live in when I needed a break away either on Business or holiday.

I do not recommend Kennels. I did trial what I thought was a good one once. When I came back only to find one very fat Beagle and one skinny Beagle .... needless to say, they were housed together!

I have many owners who take their Beagles on holiday with them. . even abroad skiing, boating or walking holidays. I took 5 down to Exmoor on such a holiday and they had the best times. Not sure I did! Especially the Cliff walks obviously all on leads! LOL!

Yes, Beagles can swim when they are mature. On the following page is Ety, she world get in and out of the pool on her own and world do so many times a day always supervised of course.

A puppy will not swim and will panic so until he/she gets his wings beware of water. I remember Prudence as a puppy out on a walk galloped over a plank misjudged it and fell into the River Arun ... quick thinking I had to go in ... . Brrrrrrrr!

Beagles will roll in smelly or dead things it's a natural instinct so do not scold them, for it is up to you, just have to get there first! Or otherwise bathe them when you get home. I have scraped many a cow pat, dead fish, Fox poo and bird off before loading into a car, remember always have kitchen roll, wet wipes and a towel in a bag ready to be used and carried in your car. While you driving and inhaling the fumes of said material, you can say to yourself 'that's a Beagle alright' and breath!

Always be aware what can be discovered on a pavement, in a park or roadside, or someone's discarded sandwiches. Plastic tops and food wrapping. Although I have never seen notes as in ££££s!

Etty loves the pool and will get in and out all day

Now lets talk about destruction.

All puppies love to chew, don't forget they are babies and have baby teeth which at around 16 weeks will drop out or be swallowed, as the adult teeth emerge. If you provide plenty of chewing healthy toys there will be less chance of gnarling on your furniture.

So, there are manufactured chews especially for this and you can find them in good pet Stores , on line and at doggy shows. I like wood objects like tree root as totally natural or the 'Antlers' full of minerals. Look on your PC for them as delivery is possible, also Amazon. We also talked about 'Kongs' with different strengths of rubber.

Yes, you probably will not escape the odd thing being damaged such as a TV Remote, shoes, trainers, glasses ... but more dangerously Wires (tv and music centre's).

Post! ! ! Yes even letters, I had a cheque through the door for £300 chewed by one of my pups! The answer to avoid all the above is up to you. Everything you love, everything dangerous and that includes food, medications and sweets must be out of puppy's way or reach.

Okay, this leads us to poisonous substances for any breed of puppy. There is a comprehensive list on the KENNEL CLUB Site but I will mention a few. Grapes, Mushrooms, Onions and chocolate, sugar substitutes, chewing gum and pain killers like Ibuprofen are all toxic to dogs ... if they are eaten, they are all killers. If this happens to your Beagle, gauge the quantity if you can, have the wrapper handy and ring your vet who will access the danger.

Best to avoid as prevention is better than cure. If toxicity levels are high he/she will have Charcoal to eat, made to throw up and be kept on a drip so your bill could be hefty, also long term damage to his kidneys and liver could result ... be aware.

Do not let your children feed him with sweets or their food, cherish your precious furkid! Eventually it will all be clearer and there will be harmony in your home and you will know what is potentially dangerous. Socks and bra's are typical Beagle theft items that partially could be swallowed, as well as tennis, ping pong balls. Surgery will be required if these have been engulfed.

I owned a goat once (ONCE I might add) who mingled with my flock of sheep and became chief as she was very bossy ... she got into my house by my stupidly, thinking she will not go in. She did ... ate all the tops of my house plants on her way upstairs and several tea towels! ! ! Yes, they appeared at the back end ... that's a Goat for you. But for a dog their gut will be blocked, can twist, die off and will need life changing emergency surgery. If you love it look after it!

Insurance!

Some veterinary surgeries will do a scheme to help you with any forward costs. Ask at reception before your puppy is home (I have always recommended taking your new puppy for a consultation within 7 days of collection and I always put this in my contracts).

As I have said before a genuine breeder will also give you 14 days Insurance cover with a respected broker. I used Pet Plan. This will cover you from the day of pick up. Obviously existing conditions will not be covered so discuss fully with your breeder. The chosen company will get in touch with you before the 14 day period expires to ask if you wish to continue.

There is a minefield of pet insurance companies so this could be researched again before purchase and costed in.

Veterinary consultations can lead to big money, so it's always wise to Insure. Take your puppy in and discuss relevant facts at your vets, the dog may have to go anyway for further vaccinations. Let the vet check the puppy over ears, eyes, heart as needed ... this way you can be sure you have chosen a well-bred dog from a reputable breeder.

If your puppy is happy, healthy and true to breed standard your vet will say' what a lovely puppy, he/she is gorgeous, nice puppy etc etc etc ... you will have peace of mind that with Insurance you are covered for most things ... but that depends on the type of cover ... it is important to read, read and read, to digest the terms of the policy and decide what is for you and your pocket!

Buy good dry dog food, the more expensive it is the better the quality. Buy cheap and you buy twice as your Beagle will prove to you with runny stools, or sickness. Go for mid-range prices you will be fine.

If you want to feed raw there are many types of raw feeding trays already prepared, raw frozen bags you can defrost or get from your local Butcher and prepare yourself. As I have said before, I used to feed raw but as my numbers increased the kitchen resembled an abattoir!

Please buy only the freshest of meats as. Yes ... bacteria can be present ... personally if you have children or expecting I world not feed raw.

Your Garden!

Of a reasonable size and not filled with trampoline's, swings or a Potager! If your garden is suitable for your children, then it is fine for a puppy as long as the following applies. Fencing secure down to the ground which is not muddy and drains well. I had professionally laid artificial grass and never looked back. It drained well, no mud, jet washed easily and because it was laid by a firm was nailed to a wooden frame thus minimising chance of it being dug up. If you have a conservatory in the garden these are great for getting your Beagle adjusted to the garden and they love sunning themselves too!

Arooooooo - ing Singing - Barking

If you have close neighbours, then all the above need to be kept in check especially in the night-time as they may not be deep sleepers and will not appreciate the noise.

Do not go to work, or out, leaving your dog in the garden especially if he/she is a noisy Beagle ... a dog flap is a great idea and your pet can choose to go in and out when he/she likes.

Obviously, you will be picking their droppings up in a hygienically double bag and depositing it in a special container for this purpose only. After washing down with disinfectant ... Always have poo bags in the house and when you go out walking ... be prepared take your rubbish home or placed in special bins provided. There is no excuse for not doing so and councils can impose heavy fines!

Doggy Toys, I will repeat as it is important ... as a priority these must be safe. You do not want to be spending ££££££'s at the vets putting your Beagle through an operation to remove objects swallowed. A plastic bottle with the top ring removed placed in a sock and tied makes a fab toy short term ... they love to crunch down on it.

Charterwood Fashionette aka Bliss

Exercising the Beagle is about mental activity as well as physical. Take a look at the toys and chews available. I have been asked lots of times about bedding, crates and where does my beagle sleep? Exercising the Beagle is about mental activity as well as physical. Take a look at the toys and chews available. I have been asked lots of times about bedding, crates and where does my beagle sleep?

Well I can say honestly never on my bed, ever. Make a den under the stairs or have a pen in the kitchen if there is room. I have never shut my Beagles in a Crate but have used them door open with Vet Bed in and a safe soft toy. Vet bed can be washed and dried very quickly as well as a dog snuggle blanket or old towel you may have.

Bizarte Cupcake ... . . my pride and joy ... .

Work out before you get your puppy where he/she will sleep, then you are prepared. Jumping or being placed on your bed he/she will hurt them self-getting down and probably mark his territory by peeing on it!

Puppies will pee anywhere full stop. Physically they cannot hold it when they are under 6 months old. After that they can be trained to go outside ... do not scold as I have said be prepared. Newspaper, pads on the floor and have wet wipes handy but never leave where your beagle can get them.

Neutering - the BIG question to be or not to be?
I recommend never do so in the Beagles first year of life. Or with the boys leave them alone if not a nuisance.

Humping your teddy or favourite pillow is all normal ... it's the hormones rising just like your teenager changes, are going on in the body. Let him have his own humping toy and do not be surprised that females can do it as well, it's all hormonal rising.

Your vet may say let's do the neutering now and tell you about cancerous risks in later life ... do not rush into it ... it does not calm them down and suddenly make them behave ... the girls wait until after the 2nd season if you are not a Breeder this will give her a better life and she will not be contained to the house when she has a season.

Season's in Bitches … … … … .

Some of this is worth repeating…

She will have an alluring odour to attract a male and she will be eager as the dog, to find a suitor! ! ! Her female parts will enlarge as well, and this is the dangerous time for walkies. She will have to stay home in the garden unless you live in the countryside and can walk early avoiding others … keep her on the lead. But be aware as a male dog can pick up her scent miles away.

I remember an occasion when I had a female in the garden whilst I was weeding, and a terrier was at our fence line digging furiously to get in … he/she had come from about 2 miles away! ! very tenacious.

If you go ahead with either male or female neutering, then book them in first thing in the morning, no food so leave them at your vets. Go about your day do not fret and when you collect them do not have a big lampshade collar on him/her. I have never ever used one and no harm was caused.

They come home and need to rest so no jumping up or down, lead exercise over the following week. Do not show you are anxious as they will read you and become sorrier for themselves, just act normally if you can.

Check the wound daily and make sure it is not inflamed or angry looking, you may have been given some antibiotics and pain relief ... . use them as instructed, if you are worried at all, then go back to your vet.

Keep to a feeding routine and do not over stuff him. Scrambled egg with rice and cooked chicken or fish (coley) are good in the early days. He/she may sleep more than usual and if a bitch, check her stitches too and if you see any pus phone your vets for advice.

Phantom pregnancy ... . or swollen teats ...

This can and often occurs when she has finished her season. It is again a hormone rush and they will go down in a week or so on their own ... Obviously, she has not been mated? ? ? One hopes.

Should your girl be pregnant or you know she has been mated accidentally then if you ring your vet he/she can give her injections (2 over 5 days) to stop any chance (hormonal) it may bring her back into season so it's all best avoided in the first instance.

The boys recover more quickly just limit the exercise to lead only for a week or so. You will know when he/she is fully recovered, may be the stitches are out now and the wound should be dry and healed.

Any wet discharge either from the Bitch's wound or the Dog's must be examined by your vet. The operation site may be compromised, and infection set in ... a dose of antibiotics will be needed.

These operations do NOT change a temperament of a dog ... it is what it is. Changes may occur from other male dogs as they are not a threat anymore to their masculinity. The risk of cancers are small but as with any organ you never know.

Chapter Ten

Out and About ... ...

You may have need to use the services of the above. You can find local services on your PC or Yellow Pages. I have used on occasion and found them very helpful. But, and it's a big but ... check them out first thoroughly.

The Day-care Centres must be clean, not over filled with other dogs also run by folk who know about breeds, training and medical instances for your peace of mind.

Dog Walkers must be Insured, CRB checked and again either have done a doggy 'First Aid' course and have the right transport and intelligence to provide a safe service --- remember yours will have to walk with other dogs so early socialisation is a must when you get your puppy.

I cannot overstate if you are going on holiday and you want to have your dog kennelled, then please check out the facilities thoroughly before committing. You do not want to be worrying that your pooch is locked up in a cell whilst you party!

There are usually plenty in your area but do not choose by location choose by function, your Beagle must have exercise, warmth and food and be under scrutiny health wise, you can then leave him knowing he/she is looked after.

Another choice is a dog sitter in your home ... again find them on your PC. A great choice if you have other animals such as cats, a horse etc and you will have peace of mind knowing they are well cared for in their own environment as well as looking after your house.

Chapter Eleven

Stories From My Life With Beagle's ...

Fortunately, I owned a house in a small Hamlet on the South Downs, a National Park. Here all my Beagles could enjoy the countryside every day running free where there was little or no traffic. I could take 6 or 8 on leads up onto the hills there they could be very much like their breed, sniffing, hunting, searching playing.

Always good, but other times they world be on 'a scent' then I world call my head off (fruitlessly as it didn't work) give in and make my way home .... I gave up worrying as it world be of no use ..... then they world eventually come home. . might be an hour could be 24 hours .... panting, muddy wet ... but tired out!

I lived on a Shooting Estate with deer everywhere and pheasants ... sometimes the deer were culled as there were so many and then my Beagles stayed on the lead.

Pheasants were abundant and I remember Dark Knight my Stud Beagle loved to chase them up into a tree.

One day he disappeared as I made my way home ... a truck appeared with Dark Knight riding Shotgun! He had a huge Pheasant in his jaws.

The Game Keeper got out ... let Dark Knight out grabbing the bird as he did so and flinging it in the back of the truck. He said 'that's 35 quid he could have cost me!' At the same time Dark Knight leaped into the back of the truck , stole the dead bird and ran off and went home.

Willow and Saffron with their Bizarte Beagle Nutmeg

One thing about a beagle I have forgotten to mention is they are tenacious and do not give up readily.

Later Pheasant casserole was on the menu and with no lead shot in it!

On another occasion I met a friend walking on the estate with her Border Collie's and a Norfolk Terrier. Mine, all of them, got on with her doggies well.
We walked together catching up with local gossip whilst unbeknown to us Dark Knight was nowhere to be seen.

Then we heard a racket ... a bleating of animals with wool on! ! ! Yikes I had no idea there was a field of sheep on the other side of the hedge ... we peered through the Beach Post and Rail (fence) ... there we could see a flock of sheep all in a triangle watched over by Dark Knight ... Argh ... they were all huddled together apart from one ewe who stood out in front stamping her foot.

Argh ... I had to get him. I called (fruitlessly). The sheep moved as he herded them as if they were a wave ... the whole keeping together for safety.

'That's it I have to get him' ... squeezed through the hedge, climbed over the Post and Rail ... believing that at any moment a farmer with a gun will come and world be angry! ! Argh ... I jumped down over the Post and Rail and landed directly on the Electric sheep wire although it did not react.

ARGH you could hardly see it ... I scrambled to my feet and ran as fast as I could to my Beagle ... he ran too and so did about 60 sheep

Argh ... finally, I cornered him with the help of a cocktail sausage put the lead on and headed back to the fence. . I lifted him over the Post and Rail and my friend reached through and grabbed him ... I climbed over the electric wire but touched it. In doing so this time I received a shock which made me leap onto the Post and Rail catching a neck chain I was wearing, it flipped up and struck me in the face.

I will never forget that occasion as when my friend and I were back together she was folded up in hysterical mirth! Really, I mean really laughing!

**

I was lucky enough through my years of breeding that I only had a few Beagles that needed to be rehomed. I think I remember 3 out of 30 years of doing so.

There was a message one day could I rehome a male that I had bred as the wife now had to go back to full time work. The Beagle was 3 now ... I said I world collect him as I had folk waiting for older Beagles to come up for re-homing.

I was also showing that day with Bliss aka Charterwood Fashionette and the venue was not too far from the home of the said Beagle. Bliss was wonderful and we had a successful show and she won in her classes.

From the showground I drove to the home of the Beagle for re-homing. Oh, I could see many a problem at the home and could plainly see why things were difficult ... there was now a huge conservatory taking up a third of the garden in which a huge Trampoline was also in situ. .
The actual garden space was minimal ... no dog could get exercise etc on that tiny piece of lawn ... anyway without further ado I left with him and with both beagles in separate crates ... guess what ? ? ?

Driving down the M23 there were major roadworks, cars were nose to tail ... speed max was 30 mph ... ... bang ... the rear car tyre blew ... Argh ... there were no hard shoulders and I placed hazards on and made my way off the tarmac.

As luck world have it camera's recorded speed and traffic conditions and I was picked up at their watch office and an array of men came to my aid ... ... they winched my car (a Honda CRV) onto their truck complete with me and the Beagles.

Once clear of the Motorway they unloaded me at the services station where I called my husband to rescue us. He came eventually, changed the spare and we made it home ... And its only Sunday ... I re-homed the Beagle to a lovely family where it could play in their garden free from restriction.

**

When selling a puppy to a family I was always very particular to whom they world go to, as these were my babes.

Sometimes when a prospective buyer world ring, I could tell whether their suitability was evident ... as I have said before, if the first question they asked was 'How Much? ' then the hairs on the back of my neck world raise ... if they had read my advertisements they world know? ? Wouldn't they?

Once into a conversation I could say quite easily that I a) had none for sale or b) had people coming to view. Learning to read people's intentions became second nature to me and I am proud of my Owners who purchased a Beagle puppy and became my friends.

I always made sure the puppy was suited to the owner and his family, it's not just about getting a sale! ! It's what is best for the longevity of the partnership between Dog and Owner.

Having Beagles has introduced me to many new people, at shows, walks, film shoots and puppy breeding. I hope I have been able to make these people happy and to achieve their goals ...

Showing ... ... your Beagle as a hobby or on a more serious level

It's a great way of socialising your puppy. They can begin puppy show training groups at 4 months or so, these are usually light hearted affairs when they are this young. Look at the KENNEL CLUB online for one near you. Go along and see what they are about and of course you will find many different breeds and ages.

Here you can find like minded people looking to train and show their furkid's. You may only want to do it as a hobby and that is fine, but the bug will bite you and who knows we may see you at Crufts!

Even the 'fun' shows have pedigree classes as well as fun elements and at the same time there are Shows held under KENNEL CLUB rules called 'Companion Shows'.

These are a great way to get your puppy out and about, also show training will teach him or her obedience and you will
gain a firmer bond with your dog.

Also let's not forget you meet some really lovely people and it gets you out and about as well. There is always that chance to gain a prize, although of course, you will always take the best dog home.

Bliss Charterwood Fashionette.

If you wish to progress, then look for 'Championship Shows' run under strict rules ... similar to 'Companion Shows'. Here you will meet breeders who show off their stock to the public and the specialist Judges.

They are usually noisy affairs with trade stands and the public looking at their favourite breeds.

Go along without your Beagle, get a feel for the show and see if you think you could give it a go, another time.

To show in the Pedigree classes your Beagle will need to be a KENNEL CLUB Registered Pedigree in the UK.

So … when you choose the breeder of your new puppy make sure they have the Papers you will need. You can check this on line at the KENNEL CLUB.

Most breeders have an Affix for their Beagles they breed, Mine is Bizarte and then the dogs name, so always ask before you go to visit their litter.

If you do enjoy showing then you will travel to various venues and it can rack up moneywise with entries and fuel costs so to start, stay within a boundary there are usually plenty of shows in the Summer.

On the day, your Beagle will have been well prepared the day before maybe bathing and trimming. He/she needs to look their smartest. You have the right lead (a loop with a lead no collar) and he/she has proved himself at Ring Craft.

Take things you will need, your entry form, receipt (entries can be done on line) wet wipe towels, poop bags, bowls for food (and for yourself) water and of course. Dress smartly no high heels or short skirts you do not want to outdo your Beagle. Find those clothes that fit you comfortably and are not distracting, you will need to step out or run on all surfaces so comfy shoes and if wet sensible brogues.

Arrive in good time after you have mapped the journey the day before. Your Beagle will need to go in a crate on the Championship Showground they can be found in specific tents. Here he/she can now have some water and periodically he/she can come out for toileting and exercise.

Find your ring, note the entrance and when you will need to be outside in the collecting area ready to enter. When it is your turn enjoy every minute.

I never go first nor last. . but that is peculiar to me. You have trained, you have watched what to do and practiced, this is your moment! If you are lucky to get a rosette well done onwards and upwards.

It is all about production on the day. Type of show, the stand, the table, the movement, it will all become easier the more you do. I showed all my horses in hand so it's not that different ... never show your sad or cross, if you think you could have done better … it's a judge's opinion on that day, go ahead and as I said onwards and upwards.

Charterwood Ensignia (Morse)

I remember the very first Championship dog show I attended. It was at Guildford in Surrey and Prudence a Tri-colour bitch puppy was bathed and prepped for the performance. I arrived in plenty of time and as I parked up a throng of people peered into the rear of the car to see what I had brought! ! ! It was rude for sure.

Later in the collecting area one chap came over and said 'this is what you have got to beat' pointing at a lovely example of a Beagle exiting his class ... Firstly, I had never met this man before, nor had I any expectations of grandeur. Again I thought how rude.

I could have run for the hills, but, really no ... I came, I saw, I conquered, so I showed Prudence and she was going really sweetly until the Loud speaker, which was ringside, squawked like a Golden Eagle and then someone had a coughing fit into the Microphone ... poor Pru, she never recovered and with her tail between her legs struggling to get free.

The lady judge fully understood and was very kind handing me a rosette ... it may have ruffled some feathers but I never gave up on showing and had some great fun times.

When we moved to Spain, I joined the KENNEL CLUB of Espana and I showed under their rules (FCI), we did not know or speak Spanish, but I managed several wins also Group wins.

It was very different to English Showing. Apart from the heat which at times was unbearable the whole style of production was on another level.

The judges could be quite rough when handling and looking in the mouth to see if the teeth were even (if you intend to show your Beagle they must have a good bite not uneven nor overshot or undershot). I will explain further in another chapter. This made me think about continuing as I did not want any of my Beagles handled like that, so I retired. Rough handling can spoil what was a very neat dog.

More about Dew claws they can be left on for showing but most breeders will have them removed. They can do them themselves between day 2-4 of the pups birth before the nervous system kicks in thus avoiding pain.

Dew claws can cause a lot of problems such as tearing, infection and may need to be removed later under anaesthesia. With some breeds they are left on purposefully such as retrievers or swimming dogs as they help with traction exiting water on banks.

The bite on the Beagle must be level so the teeth are even and not inwards nor overshot. Sometimes the Jaw can be over the bottom jaw and vice versa, as they are in the genetics these faults cannot be made good.

Your dog must have a good even bite and a good judge will want to see this when examining your Beagle on the table.

Occasionally Cherry Eye can cause a problem also a genetic fault. This is where the inner third eyelid pops out and stays out.

It resembles a cherry a red blob, and you can with a clean finger or cotton bud try very gently and push it back in under the eyeball. This should only be attempted skilfully and without roughness. The vet can also try and with a stitch it may stay in but most occasions the Cherry will need to be tacked back in under anaesthesia.

I remember visiting a kennel to look at a bitch puppy advertised for sale. It was a licenced kennel and I made an appointment. There were two girls for sale about 4 months old in a paddock and they galloped around looking like freedom had come.

One stood out from the other a very good type of dog with well-set long ears. I asked to see the mother and she joined them in the small paddock ... all looking good so far. Then I asked to see the father.

the owner showed me the KENNEL CLUB Registration and then the Stud dog joined the three in the paddock he was a stocky (somewhat over weight) tri-colour.

The man carried on chatting and then was called in to the house to get the phone. I called the male dog over and ran my hands over him looking carefully at his face. I saw much to my horror his top jaw was over his bottom jaw by easily 2 inches! ! He was also heavy in Flews, the muzzle area that covers the mouth.

As I was looking to show and breed from the girl at a much later stage this genetic fault could come to the fore in puppies so for me it was a No. We left the premises after saying our excuses and it did take me a while to let that sink in ... that some one thought it was okay to use him as a stud dog with that fault ... ... so you see care must be taken.

Obviously with even the purest pedigree dog something could arise at a later stage and it is not the fault of the dog. There are no sure-fire guarantees, you have to buy the best you can afford that has been reared and nurtured in the best possible way ... so that first visit to the Breeder is all important!

Some dogs will take to the showring and strut their stuff! Others will not enjoy it at all, so it has to be a fun rewarding experience for you both.

I often had folk say to me when looking at a puppy to buy 'Awwww but I don't want to show' … indicating either a) they don't want to pay too much or b) they don't care if it is male or female they are buying.

All thought should go into all these things before purchase and visiting the breeder. Getting a properly bred and nurtured puppy who is of show ring quality will probably be worth its weight in gold, against a sickly or spindly puppy in vets bills.

I always say this, you feed and look after the well-bred puppy which, money wise you will also gain, with the not so good puppy the outcome may be very different long term.

It may not be the breeders' fault at all, of course sometimes these things happen, but that is why I always say if you cannot afford the best then save and wait until you can.

When looking at a litter of pups I re-iterate, know in your head what you really want. Never choose on the basis of 'oh! but he/she came towards me' or 'she was hiding at the back' you need a happy, healthy puppy willing to see who you are with a wagging tail and friendly kisses. Your Beagle will be with you for years ... it is your investment!

Chapter Twelve

True Events ... ...

When I received a call for using my puppies for a Lloyds Bank Commercial from my agent who seeks animals for theatre, film, also advertising I jumped at the chance .

My agent knew I had puppies of 8/9 weeks so I agreed the venture. I had to get to London with 6 puppies so decided the best way world be by train. After boarding a London Bound Train we made it to St Pancras with a crate of Beagle pups ... we were stopped by folk wishing to know why, where , if er ... NO they are not for Sale ... . Many snaps were taken using mobile phones and at last we were in a Taxi heading for Blue Sky Studios.

Here we settled them into a play pen with toys, milk water and soft blankets. They were treated like Royalty and the filming began also photo's for banners and posters. We rested them in between shootings and there were many young people only too willing to hold and snuggle the puppies.

It was a very long day but we had a very tasty lunch and were treated very well finally leaving for our train back to Sussex, thankfully just before rush hour!

Bizarte Beagle puppies for Lloyds Bank

Eventually we had an e-mail from the LLoyds Advertising Team which showed me the posters and a video. I must mention the crochet caps the pups wore were made on the scene by a very clever lady as adjustments had to be made.

The theme was 'Join Our' so the caps conveyed this message. The advertising lasted for months and were in Lloyds Bank branches. They could be seen at Waterloo Station, the Guardian Newsaper, and posters around the country. Me one proud Mamma.

On another shoot I did, only this one was in Chelsea for the German Vanity Fair Magazine with Top Fashion Designer Roberto Cavalli who makes the most amazing gowns for women.

It was absolutely pouring with rain so the garden shoot with the models was re-located to a Pub! He came out to meet us, smoking a huge Havanna, looking at my group, 3 Beagles and me, drenched. He took the Beagle leads and posed with a tall, lean model draped over his shoulder, the blue smoke from the Cigar creating an ethereal cloud over them.

He could not speak any English and muttered something in Italian in my ear ... I gathered up the beagles before they decided to scarper ... in a puff of smoke Roberto had disappeared back into the pub for me my drive home.

Mr Morse (drawn by me) aka Charterwood Ensignia

I never gave it a thought until a few weeks had passed and I casually mentioned to my husband I had driven over strange markings on the road in Chelsea.

Now remember I'm a country girl so had taken no notice. Ah, slight problem apparently it is a charge area, so a fee has to be paid ... really yes! It was only £12 but if you did not pay it then it jumped, and you could end up paying hundreds! Whoops ... . I paid it online- what a cheek ... they should be paying me! ! Ha ha !

After that episode I had the call to take One Beagle to East Sussex to a pad that was once Led Zeppelins old house, yes, an old Stately home. It was for another German Magazine come Catalogue showing designer clothes.

When I got Mr Morse out of the car he had vomited ... so as I was always prepared with wet wipes, poo bags and kitchen roll, water and towels I managed to clean up but there was a definite odour lingering.

The shoot was in the garden and a thousand rabbits had obviously used the lawn as a toilet! ! Well Mr Morse aka Charterwood Ensignia was head down derriere up!

A sylph like skinny lizzie appeared in gorgeous flowing robes her skin glowing my mouth dropped ... me in Denims and Cowboy boots!

I showed her how to trot him out and he moved beautifully . . but when she took the lead his nose was on the grass ... she tried several times and in the end they got the shots they wanted. By now he was getting bored of going over the same ground.

I was there about 20 mins with Mr Morse who still had a smell of rotting compost about him, I took the cheque, 'thank you very much' and we departed, the smell in the car lingered so I drove back with the window down a tad

.

Bizarte Adamant ... . .

Words and Initials explained

Ringcraft **-** training so your puppy is ready to enter a ring under a judge.

Kibble **-** dry dog food bought usually by the sack or bag.

Tracker - worn on the dogs collar to show where about of the dog

Antlers - real deer antlers for teething dogs or as chews

Kong **-** a hollow rubber toy that can be filled with tasty stuffing

Potager - area of garden to grow your own fruit and veg.

UTI - 'Urinary Tract Infection'

NCCD - Neonatal Cortical Cerebellar Degeneration' a genic disease-causing damage to movement

FCI - 'Federation Cynologique International'.= World Organisation of KENNEL CLUBs

Carpal Valgus - genetic disorder causing Queen Anne legs where the feet point outward like a sea lion.

Thundershirt **-** a T-shirt made of Lycra made especially for dogs.

Cone **-** a plastic collar like a lampshade

CH **-** 'Champion' or champion show.

Thank you too to Percy Chattey Author, publisher and distinguished gentleman friend who helped me to produce this book.
Susan McNeil

Percychatteybooks

Story Telling (R)

Somerset House

6070 Birmingham Business Park

Birmingham

B37 7BF

Registered Number 2299335

Produced and published in the Hondon Valley, Southern Spain

Printed in Great Britain
by Amazon

44085667R00059